SWIMMING TOWARD ITHACA

Richard Tagar

POEMS

(1975-2015)

There is the moment

Swimming toward

Whale-backed Ithaca

And

The moment

On the white beach

After

CONTENTS

Early Days

Early Days

(1975-1978)

FROST

The nights draw in
Enclosing the countryside with fossil jaws.
The ice-plated ponds and streams lie paralysed all day
The wan sun
Fails even to soften the earth's rimed crust at noon

Fallen leaves,
Now nothing more than brittle flakes of crystal-water,
Crunch beneath one's feet,
Rustle like ancient warrior's arms,
Hung up in reverence by some barbarous grave,
Chafing as storm-blown sabres in a numbing breeze.

The frost lies thick
Beneath the diamond stars,
Covering the turgid mud,
Forming concrete ridges
Where yesterday there was slush.

The night draws in,
Tightening its unimaginable hold on the sleeping land,
Crushing life between fossil jaws;
And over the bare bones of nature,
The feral, the fanged wind, sighs.

TWILIGHT

The old man with

The great white

Beard

Sunken eyes

Wrinkled face

Wearing a Panama hat

A cigarette in his

Mouth

On the flickery

Old film

A palette and brushes

In his hand:

MONET!

Half-blind and

Near to death

But still painting

Eighty-six years old

Lost in his work

Among the lily-ponds

Of Giverny!

'POP GOES THE EASEL'

(Ken Russel, 1962)

The black and white film
'from the archives'
The young women with
The Jean Shrimpton hair-
Styles and faces
Men in drainpipe trousers
And short hair:
The Pop-artists
At the fairground.

Yes,
They *were* so like
Children
Amongst their picture-
Postcards, newspaper-
Clippings of Marilyn Monroe
And flashing lights of
Electronic gaming tables
'Twisting'
On the dance-floor
Very aware that it's
All on film
Fifteen years ago.

Ave atque vale!

Walt Whitman when

Will they bury you

In the ground

And

Forget you ever

Wrote poetry?

Scientific Socialism

No speeches, please!

Too easy to applaud

The dull rhetoric of

The MANIFESTO... appealing

To hearts which had no time

For heads, but who

Applauds

The precise (quiet) accents of

Science, which does not

Accept every dotted 'i' ;

Follows the staling track

(wrested with life's labour)

Through the dark

Thorn patch?

POSTCARD

I have written a post-

Card to you, who

(in imagination)

I have slept with, whose

Every inch I have

Tasted only in my dreams, with-

Out any reason to think that you

Yourself wish anything of the sort,

Yet I have written in Comradeship, tho'

With an eye to the future.

For: B.G.

A fringe of brown hair

Showed under the

Emerald scarf, revealing

Your small ears, with the

Golden, double-stud sleepers.

Your

High cheekbones and oval face,

The large enamel butterfly-

Brooch on your right

Breast.

But

It was the unblinking, open,

Grey eyes which so

Dazzled me!

Resurgam?

No

EPITAPH!

Ashes only as

Seed scattered all

Down the wind.

EPIPHANY 1.

Burnt-orange

The wall

A-pattern (pale)

With

White light.

Love poem No. 1-?

Trust me;

I will not loose your hand in darkness;

By this know me.

English summer

I am excited

For the day

(cloudless and hot)

Has been the

First among many

Wet and dull and

The twilight brings

No sign of

Gathering clouds!

Postcard from Finland

Today,

A postcard,

(quartered),

Showing a lake,

Calm with

Rocky islands and trees;

A narrow wood bridge with

One rail among reeds;

Through pine-trees a stretch

Of water;

On the shore, farm-buildings;

The reedy-edge of a lake,

Green shade of trees, shelt-

erring a wooden boat pulled

onto the grass:

On the back of this,

I have written that

It has rained but now

The sun shines,

That I have rowed

All afternoon and

Will swim later, and

That we shall go on

North for the weekend.

Gull Flight

The black-backed
Gull, moving its
Head jerkily,
Quickly, from side
To side, beak
Outstretched, eye
Yellow, glancing,
Searching for fish
Over the wave-tops
Adjusting unconsciously
Minutely, the set
Of wings, leading-edge,
Flight-feathers and
Tail-attitude,
Seeing now how far
Fallen behind the ship,
Beats swiftly,
Deliberately, beak
Up, swings out,
Circles in over
The wake, now drawing
Level with the wheelhouse.

On Deck

On the

Green deck

A red deck-

Chair

The grey sea

And the mist,

The sun

Behind clouds

The mist

Spits water

And

The sea

Is,

As far as

Can be seen,

Empty.

Soviet Trawler

A black-hulled

Trawler, grey

Upperworks,

Rusty,

A dirty

Red flag

Difficult to see

At the masthead

But

She has too many

Antennae, too much

Radar and

Moves too fast to

Be fishing.

Tempus fugit!

The alarm-clock ticking

Very loud, very

Regular

And the rain has made

The grass

Wet outside the window.

Still Life

On the white table

A round, squat

Glass vase

Two-thirds filled

With water

In it large faded daisies

Blue cornflowers

And tall

Pyramid-shaped clusters

Of small yellow

Flowers, white blossoms

And green, purple-

edged grasses with

furry thick

seed-heads.

Electric storm over Lake Paijanne

A sudden loud

Thunderclap

Over the still

Wide lake

The low

Grey clouds

Which have

Gathered

Unnoticed pour

Hailstones

Into the woods

A

Zig-zag of lightning

Over the

Swaying treetops, the

Wind

Hisses in the pine

Branches,

The leaves of the

Silver birches

Rattle.

Sunrise on the lakes

From

Behind the trees a pink

Glow

Which colours the under-

Parts

Of clouds, a yellow at

The base of the pine trunks,

The

Glow a rose glaze upon

Dead

Still waters, the mist

Moves

Out from the damp shore

Six

Feet deep, cold; fish

Jump

Terns crying skim

Over

The surface matched

By

Their reflections

In

The earliest light of

Day.

I am very tired

(my eyes feel raw

and keep closing)

I should have gone

To bed...but just

Had to wait up

For the sunrise.

The Fly

The fly

With long legs

And

Thin outstretched wings

On the

Window, black

Ag-

ainst the un-

focussed

background of

pine

and birch.

Too late

I talked,

Yes... of Socialism

Amid the after-

Dinner drinks

(the managing director had...

perhaps

drunk more than he should)

directors' wives

sipped red liqueur, sang

sad peasant

songs in the

pale blue . dawn .. ,

factory chimneys streaming white smoke

trails .. ..

The

fig-

ure of

a

yacht

edge on

to the

breeze

just like

a raz-

or blade

so fine

half

twist-

ed

leaning

into the breeze

Country Life

(1979-1987)

Late Autumn

The bare, grey frame

Of the tree,

    Where

A few leaves –

    Yellow triangles –

Stream out

    In the fresh wind;

One by one,

    Fall,

Spinning in their fall.

Two days –

      or perhaps three –

All the limbs of the tree

    Will be quite clean

Of their pennons –

Winter evening

There is a landscape

Beyond my window

Of black, stirring

Lattice-work of winter trees

Against a fading sky

Of blue-grey

The hour of dusk –

Single lights prick out

The rough contours of the land;

Above the horizon, pass,

Twist, melt, shape-shift

Clouds

The colour of an

Ink-wash ...

There is no sound.

Fish Tank

The strong woman-scent of your armpits

When you bend – net in hand –

To the fish tank.

I want so much

To reach through their moist fur

And slip your loose breasts

Into my hands

Clearings

You in a white, belted dress

With your breasts raised —

For once —

In a bra and

Your chestnut hair

Down your long back

    *

I had got you to try

On the straw boater: -

It slants across your hair,

Frames your dancing brown eyes

    - Across the rainbow of memory
       This bright image beckons

    *

He had asked —

Teasing in his embrace

    - "Are you a girl?"

" 'course I am,"

(a downward glance)

"*they* ain't gnat-bites."

SIESTA

"It is not that I love you less,

Than when before your feet I lay,

But to prevent the sad increase

Of hopeless love, I keep away."

(Edmund Waller)

But in the foetid dark upon some stranger

Bed

Your eyes are rising like a doubled sun;

And there I twitch and sweat

And blast the fate

That strangers us;

And will not let me my hands fill

With your breasts, mouth hot-press

Upon your living throat;

And will not let you in your cool

Hands take my aching lust,

Nor

Uncurl yourself to me.

SHEEP

You and he are burnishing in the white

Greek light, turning to Bacchus

And Ariadne; you sleep curled,

Pards nestling at the bed's foot.

I marshal my charges, conduct

The daily roll-call of the sheep,

Push *Dopey's* head out of the bucket,

Half-filled with pellets, check for 'fly',

Watch the thistles grow in wild pasture

And dark clouds scutter like this flock.

How?

How to tell this skinny girl,

Seated here at the kitchen table

- She whose sex-life is all
Wrapped up –

That you might just

Love her?

Dreamt kisses!

Dreamt kisses on my mouth,

Dreamt hands' circling shoulders,

Dreamt breasts warm through clothes. . . .

Dreaming I kissed you,

Waking knew you

Slept with him.

The frame outside time

Slips:

She is not there to steady the

Peerless temple with her bright flesh.

She is not there, will not come;

I love her

But she loves him: -

I cannot, quite, feel jealousy

For her happiness in his

Embrace

Dear diary...

Dear diary, what's to be done?

Y'see, my neighbour's banging

The girl I want

    -   No joke -

I can hear them through the wall

(if I press my ear up close).

It's just not fair – hello,

She's having fun – the swine, I'll

    -   Bloody hell! -

No woman moans like *that*,

Not so long, not even in the movies,

(not in the one I saw)

All quiet again.

I'll win her off him, somehow,

    -   I bloody will -

Diary, y'know it's really rotten luck,

I like her, as well as wanting her

To fuck!

Deep Dean

Deep Dean hollows the high Downs

Stretches a giant's sleeve

Into distant blue

Chalk's gorse-mantled

Throned in cowslips' thrilling bells

Wind-stroked the sheep-bit turf

Hic Salta! – here dance butterflies

Swerve Islamic-winged swifts

Above air-filled deeps

Solitary the ruined farm, wind-breaking

Court bristling with sentinel nettles

Owl-haunt and bat-haven its flint

Over chalk's lip, engines and bitter argument

Deep Dean fresh as world's morning

Exhales to the plane-less heaven

Leaf-like

      Unfurls.

Elegy upon Rosamund Du Clifford

Madame, ye ben of beaute shrine.

Silk hangings turned half in candle-guttering breaths

    Above her tomb

As if some prized martyr lay beneath

    That nunnery pavement

Arced now by no arch but the blue, crow-echoing sky

    Where the Trout Inn overlooks the Thames

And Carroll spun out his tale upon the water

As fer circled is the mappemounde

So wide Curtmantle's realm: England to Aquitaine

    King of the World

Henry by the Grace of God or Courtesy of the Devil

    Kneels in the gloom

Incense wreathes the Sisters' low chant

    Tears are falling, more than fell for Becket

Under the Brothers' meted lashes

For as the cristal glorious ye shyne

Through the veil that face pearled from the well

    Gushing out of earth

In squared marble arrayed, with talking elms

    Her crystal bath o'ercanopied

Like Eden's rivers flowing, She Eve and He Adam

    At the Labyrinth's heart mazed in

Paradise without the Serpent

And lyke ruby ben youre chekes rounde

And your belly, breasts, shoulders, bum

    Gleaming like Diana's

At the Fount of never-failing Youth

    And your hair

Sparkling diadem outrayed

    Like locket-chains of Saracen gold

By your pealing laughter flung to Heaven

I am trewe Tristram the secounde

Mournful incense recalls the pleasuring scents

Of perfumed chambers

Woodstock's bower-shrine to My Lady

Bedded in swansdown, young again

By Her Grace, who loved me on silk

Now silken-shrouded like a moth

Thogh ye to me ne do no dalliaunce

Nor never shall again, Rosamund,

Crowned in Death

My living heart's Queen, rose in the garden

Of Courtly Love

Famous-protectress, embalmed with Henry's Grief

World's flower, *Rosa-Mundi*

Rose of the World

Fair Rosamund!

POLAND

The country through a window,

Oak frame to its gold and green,

A view of landscape without people.

Poland's open plain is not empty, cities not stage-sets

Its people make their presence felt.

"Our people" – that phrase,

Redolent of ownership – it stinks!

"Our people, our country"

Rolls like nature off smooth tongues,

Which dare claim this narrow vision

Patriotism – the insolence astounds.

Our people, of which we are part,

Fill the mental landscape

Of our politics, remind us

How fragile is the power of

Our rulers, how lightly

May it be shrugged to naught.

History's quite alien to England,

Academics paint their grey-in-grey,

Populists erect an antiquarian Triumph

To Empire's rotten corpse –

"Cheer, you unpatriotic bastards,

We ruled the World, y'know!"

History lies deep-frozen in Poland's soil,

Keeps alight the lamp of Liberty,

Permits no forgetfulness of Rights,

Enfolds a Nation's struggle,

A struggle to be reborn:

"Poland is not lost!"

Keep the lamp of History lit;

The country you seek is in the People's eyes

   -   Or it is nowhere

Fear the rulers, that you may the better

Ensure their ultimate destruction;

Remember: England is not lost!

Visions from a window: March 1984

The vista recedes, green-brown,
Range after range of Wealden hedgerow,
Trees, heath; stippled with a white
House, a tv-mast; layer succeeds
Layer, to the bare-straggle branches
Where, grey at the edge of skyed-ice, clouds –
Airship to the silvered fin – are heavy
With the green sea's issue.

March – after the Leap-Year's intercalation –
Along the brown wood, filling with white blossom,
Rebound the pealing yaps of Sunday dogs;
Towards evening the edges of trees turn pink,
The paths grow quiet, crocus from base saffron
Transmutes to blazing gold; the river gargles low
Across the shingle, light – sparkling – pierces the
Culvert's tunnel, threads through its needle's eye.

What visions of rootedness steal ambushwards,

Soft-footed, turn up leaves from damp death?

Dreams of which England — and where? —

Stream as midges, sun-caught, to nibble

At my scalp? Nature is of ourselves, as we are

Of Nature; grub up the hedgerow with steel teeth

And drive them blind through your own flesh,

Heedless, mangle life, without a care.

Was it vulgar homesickness drove the War-Poets,

Aching in Flanders, to bring to mind such

Woods and fields? I met a woman with a dog

Mid-path: "I am afraid of another war."

What yearning burst from Elgar, when Boult

Wrung the 'Nobilmente' themes to cracking-point?

Was it nostalgia, or a vision of some perfected

England, breaking through?

Sussex: March 4th 1984

LILLITH SONNETS

(I)

Shall I angle for your likeness
In the spring's raw bursting
 Out?

No, your svelte image belongs
To candle and to log-light.
Pope, Emperor and Scythe-bearer
Open a pasteboard arc at your feet

Dark Lady Lillith of the white skin
Your hair falls Levantine about your
Throat and grows – I pray –
Coarse where limbs with trunk are
 Joined.
This sonnet finds out your shape
Yet masks its name.

(II)

"I love you"; that's a pretty

 Hollow

Nothing to whisper at the pearl-

Mother gate to you heart!

It's a robber's mask conceals

Lust for both those wet-lipped valves

That yield a sweeter entrance.

"I like you"; that somehow

Enfurls a greater truth.

Corrupt insight would smile,

Dulcet quiz: "and you don't fancy her?"

Yet surely there's more in this

 Less

Than meets a cynic's eye?

"She's got a lovely body, but..."
It's true your face is not the classic oval;
A nose upturned is owlish framed in steel;
 Yet
Lillith's, like Athena's, owl makes wisdom
Emblematic as the double-fish, swimming
Golden at your throat.

And Tomboy clothes, hands fast on hips,
As you demand respect, will not –
For any male – a plaything be...
 Still
I'm drawn to the butterfly 'broidered
On your thigh and cannot but dream
Your arms, douce, about me.

(IV)

Is Love's Progress measured in the spreading
Angle
Of a compass-pair, or hands' touch on
Skin-surface, at the warm, pointed breasts
Where heart-beats strong within this
Translucent envelope;
On the smooth orbs
Of a shapely arse?

It's not the depth (may it *be* deep!)
Which I hope to be steeped in flesh,
Nor even scent of sweet arms about me;
These are warm breath melted on cold air
To that glowing core, Lady of the cards,
Gives
Itself, in bodily affection, Substance.

(After Wm. Shakespeare)

Composition in Black, White and Scarlet

That cream throat flowers

Out the sweater's coal calyx

And her eyes also –

Slaying me suddenly –

Are dark diamonds

With sable lashes parasol'd.

Last, the hair –

Like a black cat's liquorice

And russet brindle –

Caresses a Carrara brow,

Cradles this cheek of pearl,

Backdrops your fire-bright mouth –

"Mine eyes dazzle!"

St. Luke's summer

Stealing in, blust'rous and

 Under cover of darkness,

Stealing the tatterdemalion bunting,

Winter's boistering, brute zephyr

 Leaves autumn's ash

 Naked as an emperor

Her Dress

Your dress hangs from the door:

  Sometimes the wind

  Gently stirring it,

Fills me with an apprehension it must

  Fill with your warm body,

  Walk from the door and,

  At the window, turn to me

Spitfire

Edged proud against the azure's

Upper-depth, their ellipses cut

The clouds' white evolutions

Green-eggshell wings glitter hawk's eyes

  Roll and flash the Perspex bubble –

As turns gold-brown and dull-green

Soil beneath, sprawls alike her topsides

  Arcs this ghost-solitary

Above the swimming earth

Scipio

Coward!
I know & bite my tongue
  In self-reproach
Who did not speak &
Let the moment slip;

Fool also, who could not –
  Like African Scipio –
Have the wit, falling facelong
To seize the soil &, with it,
  The hour, crying:

"Teneo te …"

I knew it was her!

I knew it was her;
From across the street
I knew it was her at the bar:
That classical head, poised;
The long white cigarette –
Making a sixth, marble, finger.

The dusk made that framed vision
Glow against the shrouding walls
Starlight fell through me
I had no words.

Queen Jane

Queen Jane poses with a cigarette:

"I'm not a morning person, really,"

        She laughs

Trips, high-heeled and short-shorted

Her over-lengthy and more than slender

      Limbs along the pavement

Souvenir

Jade-green hangs the Gaelic cross

Of veined Irish marble;

Nestles in that Mother-of-Pearl

Hollow of your throat

I so much want to kiss, then

Slip this mouth to your heart:

Hangs there, the lover's gift

He bought.

MALLAND

In the shadow of a hollow-cheeked
Bronze colossus, the bus queues form
Behind glass walls, sheltered
From the rain.
Times without number, I have made one
Of their number.
Verdigris tears streak the plinth
On which he stands, mingle with the smears
Of years leaching from the plaques
Which name: "Our Glorious Dead."

How many of us have filled the empty minutes
Reading that hard list, washed with the cold rain?
What a small thing Remembrance is,
How soon the dumb dead have faded!
Shall we wear 'Falklands Poppies'
On Armistice Days to come,
Blood-petals to embalm the memory of those
Laid, zipped in plastic bags,
In some corner of a Falklands field
Which, (others claim), will be forever Argentina?

The Armada, swallowed in the darkness

Of its unsleeping; the images that the mind retains:

The green-lit hangars, luminescent screens,

Whirring of mindless, purposeless,

All-too-pointed weaponry.

No war without loss:

'Coventry' – lost with her cross of nails

From that city's husked cathedral;

An eye for an eye – Coventry avenged

With Dresden's firestorm;

The brooding angel of Dresden's torn cathedral

Leans out against the backdrop of that murdered city.

Now Dresden is in a faraway country

Of which we know little;

We prepare to end war by preparing for war

And slide, at once, to war's end and World's-end.

Shall we let that weathered angel

Lean its sad smile over all the cities

Of Europe?

What price is too high to pay?

Is there no limit to the masochism

Of our people?

Inverted showers of Red, White'n Blue

Balloons, Elgar's disowned Pomp and Circumstance;

What could it mean to those who burned

Within a floating tomb,

Those who 'came home',

A ghastly, flag-draped cargo

Cradled in the gentle embrace of a dockside crane?

What a small thing memory is!

Let us not forget them:

The young bulls, whose blood filled the pit;

Sacrificed that Britannia's ghost

Might be conjured from Hades.

(Spring 1982)

'A Woeful Ballad to his Mistress' Eyebrow'

I write this to your eyebrow,

As Shakespeare's Jacques recommends;

Like his 'youth' I am a lover,

Like himself a melancholy man.

I'm not writing this because

Your eyebrow's more lovely

Than many another of its kind;

It is, however, peerless

Because it is your own

And crowns your spangling

      Eye.

'Triple foole'

'Why do you do things for me?'
    - A quizzical look -
What answer is possible
For me to offer, which
Would you believe?

"Because I like you?"
    - You wouldn't wear that -
'Because you fancy me, more like;
Well, you can forget it!'

"Because I love you?"
    - Most fantastical and most true -
Yet all three are true and each
Stands on its own.
Since you don't feel the same
Shall I, playing all three,
Oberon-like commission my Puck
To fetch me 'love in idleness',
Anoint your eyes that I may
To your proud Titania
Beloved as Bottom be?

Your Face

Your face through the dull type

Of these arcane pages,

A swimmer's bursting

Like a rounding bubble up

Through the water's filmy surface

  Erupts.

Hair, cheeks, eyes –

The paper dissolves,

    Satined water ripples

      - Rise up; lips nudging

Your mouth opens and my thought's

  Erased.

Wild cherry: spring

Fire in the dusk

Blossoms from bare sticks,

Burns white;

In the twilit valley

A triple star flares

Acetylene-strong

Above the clammy meadow;

Glows against the stark backdrop

Of naked trees.

Why these tears?

Why these tears,

At what do you stare

So fixedly?

Why this clutching

At photographs,

Impassive fragments?

A smile, shutter-frozen,

Caught in amber,

Documents your loss.

What good is this ritual

Shuffling of cardboard,

Inanimate, spiritless?

Why these tear-stains,

What of him you love

Will this bring back to you?

The silent world of dreams

Why do you come to me
In a dream and I
Unable to make you hear me
As if behind glass, and you
Speaking the while with another?

Why bring that look to me,
When, turning at last,
You ask what it is that I want,
Annoyed at my disturbing
Your conversation?

Why do you bring
Your slender body
To my sleeping sight,
When I may not touch nor hold you
But beat upon the glass only
And cry out to you
In the silent world of dreams?

Mayfield church resumed

(In homage: Robert Graves 1895-1985)

The tree's tip breaks through,
  Upheaves paving-slab and iron tomb-plate;
Sinuous belly-dancer, She,
Reaches to caress the polished vault,
Then fill, then burst its oaken
  Sepals.

  Transfixed, the congregation gapes,
Plump flesh turns parchment
On dry, calcined sticks;
The vicar, pop-eyed, thick-necked,
From his moss-clotted pulpit, ashes
  Falls.

  Roof broken like boiled egg,
Birds among redundant piers argue,
Echo, shake droppings into rotten pews;
This infidel ruin's with a soft,
Sappy light brim-filled, Her dominion, She
  Recalls.

Benjamin's grave

(Elegiac stanzas after Goethe & Brecht)

No pear-tree shades your grave
   Nothing more miserable
Than this death in exile
   Estranged from your books
 Your prized Klee stuffed in a suitcase
At the Bibliothèque Nationale.

At root cut off from those positions
   Which you sought to defend
Gentle Minotaur dragged to the light
   From the cool labyrinthine city:
 Berlin, West, West; Surreal Paris;
Whose stones fed, Christ-like, your imagination.

Enshrined within a splendid reliquary
   The temple of your works
Your reputation stands beyond harm
   At this last ditch
 'Ermattungstaktik' failed you
From winter, finally, this mound protects you.

Mawgan Pydar

From a car window:
Celandine and Primrose break
From an earth interstice, crumbling
Out of herringboned slate,
  Over-tussocked,
Which hems this twisting,
  Climbing lane.

  This
Lane climbing
Out of the tourist Duchy
  Dazzle-fades,
Is steeped and lost
In that deep Dozmary Pool
Not-rippled, still present
  Your face.

Midonz

Will you be mine? –

Let's have no "mine" and "thine"

Here! –

  Are you another's? –

Who may confine or possess

You? –

  I've walked round you –

Smirking like a juggler,

Huh! –

  The psyche of Earth's greening

Melds you with the wild

Cherry –

  What will I do? –

Will this fade as blossom

Falls?

In the Botanic Garden, Oxford

Ich Liebe Dich!

By the stone basin where, plashing

A duck and drake compete for our

Dropped morsels.

These plants are like you, exotics:

By the rinsed light of that milky planet

They must seem like Rousseau's

Imaginary forest.

If a more larger gulf wide-gaped

Between this charmed garden and that place

Which is focussed in your present presence

It would be the same;

Were it the moon, not gravel, but dust

Beneath my feet, that planet aquamarine,

Dusted with icing-sugar clouds, instead above,

Nothing would have changed.

In a far land, beneath this fern,

I dream of you; within the envelope

Of Magdalen's carillon, I sit in the

Botanic Garden:

Loving you!

In childhood

In childhood the grey cabinet

Stood over my bed; 'Sooty',

With a magic wand, snapped

Off to a mere stump, glowed

Through the nights I cowered

Form demons, monsters, shadows – paralysed.

Day brought back the stern

Red-Indian faces of the wall-

Paper, cardboard heads of 'Big-

Game' (courtesy of Kellogg's

Cornflakes). All that time

I was alone.

Bustle – the town

She, running for the bus,

Tries to dodge me and I her:

Unhappily we both turn

Into the same angle – collide.

She, grimacing, catches,

I think, her bus:

I move on, parting through

The bustle – irritated.

Geometra Papilionaria

This Large Emerald

                    Geometrida

Hangs

       Shred-winged

                         Off the corkscrewed

                         Glutinous fly-paper

                         Lured by the light

                         Cruelly trapped

       Liquorice-curled

Stiff

                         Proboscis

       Sipped your death.

Cryptic verses on a nocturnal storm

Racks penumbral

Occult

Moon's white-bone face

Air's tensed static

Tree's alive with chirruped

Unease.

Lightning crimps

Templing

Oak-shafts enlighten, sussural

Leaves give voice

Lowering nimbus tympanic extrudes

Moisture …

Forbidding weeping

Alas! John Donne

That they which followed

Thee could not see thy

Method's method

Was not to make

By strange device

The colours of

The butterfly's

Wing, but to translate,

There as 'twas found

Fallen upon the

Clean page the

Light, reflected, which its

Own colours shed.

I was born in the eleventh year

Of the peace.

Throughout the world

There was war.

When I was knee-high to a grasshopper

The grass was neck-high to me

At eleven years old the grass

Now waist-high

And I watched the wars

At supper-time

Heard the litany of names

Which spelt death.

Now the grass is grass-high

I'm used to it.

In the thirty-eighth year of the peace

Throughout the world

There is war

City Lights

(1988-2015)

Medallion

In the street each woman's

   Step holds an echo

Of your stride

Every chin uptilted mocks

   Your Medici-medallion's

Sharp profile;

From these womanly shards

   I build your image

In my heart.

Fear and trembling

I fear you:
As one can fear only the beloved
I fear you.

Against enemies, against oppressors,
Fear rises up, transmuted to
Defiance or to
The stubborn will to endure:

Against such fear
Revenge quenches, survival outwears;
Against you – nothing!
For I cannot take up arms
Against my love.

Yiddisher singer

Strange!

That in so many tongues

Sounds melodious as its song:

'Nachtigall',

               'Rossignol',

Latin 'Luscinia',

Loveliest of all;

Touching that

Pathos Keats could not:

Solo-vej,

           Solovej!

The Future-Imperfect

Have you walked in that other

City of Vienna;

Hearing the sublime music of Schoenberg

Penetrate the traffic's chaos,

Writing at Café Centraal

Along with Altenberg's dummy,

Anatomising flesh with Schiele,

Form with Loos (or Wagner),

Mind with Doktor Freud?

I have walked there with the Dead:

  Sunt lacrimae rerum.

River

We on this bank

They on that

The bridge's broken back.

Jade-green froth

The torrent hurtles

    Loud below.

We on that bank

They on this

  The sundering river

    Flows between.

Provençe: le vieux Château

The shutters unfurl
The tower's filled with this morning's
Hibiscus brightness.

Surprised, the green lizard
Streaks over the well's worn stone mouth
Where the green moss droops.

The eye's drawn across pantiles
To that shimmering vision of oaks,
Which are surely from Giorgione.

Light flows

Light

Flows across the door-sill

Greek

Honey with fresh yoghurt

Breaks

My fast but brings

Wasps!

Between us there is ..?

Wineglasses catching

A salty sparkle

Mimic a surface shudder

Reflect hazel laughter

  Drinking deep

    I fall

        Into

           Your

              Space.

Antwerp café

I have walked in these streets,
  I have sat in these cafes;
Have stirred away at stone tables

  My life

My love

  To the deepest, most bitter,

  Dark

  Dregs.

Café *la Terasse,* Brussels

(Composé a table le 16 Janvier 1997)

On a corner of the Celtic Lane

January sun warms me through the pane

Bankers prattle €uros

I stir my onion-soup unseen

Attempt to kill the hours in between

One appointment and the next

Try hard not to think of sex

Or love, or both, in vain.

Brussels with old maps

The tram doesn't run there now

That bus-line's changed

Route, number, destination

That bijou *square's* new

But tram and bus still ride

To fabulous ends:

Konkel,

Hunderenveld,

My favourite –

Silence/Stilte;

Imagine that –

The tram to *silence!*

Two stations of the Metro

Brits laugh at bilingual Brussels

"Oh! – Look: *Parc/Park* –

Ha, ha, ha!"

But the Welshman had it right:

You've stayed too long in town

If

Kunst/Wet station

Doesn't raise a grin.

Three Sisters

About the table

And about

Spinning fates –

Green dales

And

Wild fells,

Byronic men

And wretched girlhoods –

Scritch, scratch

At the pane,

Glossy as midnight ice,

The younger pauses,

Peers into

Black nothing

Beyond –

A child's spirit

Keening like

The wind –

Let me in,

Let me in!

The collection

Growing older

The centre of your collection's

Gravity shifts

Past an

Indefinable

Tipping-point

Life's equation's

Overturned:

No longer

Friends living

The greater number

But

Friends dead.

In the presence

(on the sofa)

There's a force-field

Forfends my touch

As if you

Were more Goddess

Than mere woman

As if touching

Were taboo.

Slipping'n sliding

No, really
Slipping on personas
(or should that be personæ?)
Isn't like slipping on bananaskins
(which were really shit unseen)
It's a question of ...
Slipping the cord over your head
(then they'll let you in, you hope)
Smiling, chatting, cajoling
(in this role, on a roll?)
Slipping off the badge and sloping off
(after the show)
It's a question of presentation
(really!)

The 30th January at Piskarov Memorial Cemetery

Bayonets upheld on polished heels

   Snowflakes crisply wreathe

The president's white hair

   Before this flame.

   Meanwhile,

The chequered forest waits.

Flow

You gotta run,

    Child,

When the ice cracks;

Hop, skip and jump,

    Child,

When the ice breaks!

Manhattan: The Fall

That broken stump
  Tooth in your
Skyline's skyscraper
  Grin

New York,
      New York,
            New York

(11 September 2001)

Perran sands

This the ended beginning

  Wet sand between toes

The Great Ocean's shuttered

   Hiss and roar

Falling from St. John's

Chapel Angarder's

  Sphinxless rock

Slice-of-lemon sky wedged

   Between

Clouds of slate

   And

Sea of pewter

   Here

The sepia past

   And

Mouthless future.

(W.M.G. 1908-2003)

The Manchester dandy

The fag-end of Victorian England

A Manchester dandy

Swings his cane

Off to the Music Halls

Before he wore khaki

For King and Country

Before the eagles were torn

Down from the walls

He died in his bed

In the age of the

Balance of Terror

Where hair-trigger response

Left no margin for error

I'd like to tell him:

Grandpa, the Iron Curtain

Was lifted, the Wall fell

In Europe's Wonderful Year

There was no more Soviet Menace

Nothing to fear

In the New World Order instead

We face a Clash of Civilisations

And mounting tallies of dead.

Grandpa, I'd like to conclude

These lines,

Asking: are we condemned

Forever to live in such

Interesting times?

Im Wunderschönen Monat Mai

Cold for the first of May

The wide streets empty

As it should be

And

Red just blurring

Dry

Sticks of copper-beech

In the park.

After drought

After drought
At long last days
Of rain sweep leaves
Through towers
Of Flemish lace

Amid the storm
This warmth
This bed
These hearts
Your face

At long last Love!
Let the wind blow
Let it rain
Let it snow
So long as mine
Your lips taste!

The Neanderthal's lament

Homs talk, talk

High voices

Like birds

Skinny things

Don't hunt

Won't last long

Not here

Hungry

I'll go kill and eat.

The scorpion's way

I am the scorpion

Lives in the cracks

This is my wall

Leave me be and

I'll do you no harm

Bother me and I'll sting

The scorpion am I!

Present Imperfect

(Aprés Charles Baudelaire: 'Á une Passante')

To the middle-aged woman

Passing the window

Of this café:

That hair,

Now grey and short and neat,

Did you wear it once

Long and lustrous and dark?

Your eyes,

Now with crow's-feet crinkled,

Did they sparkle, big and brown?

That nose,

Now sharp and tipped in red,

Did it wrinkle with delight

And make

Some young man's

Heart race?

Are you

She and am I he,

That loved and lost you then?

As for you ...

(the drunk men's verses)

As fer you,

Yer snobby, Oxbridge cunt ...

- *Kent, it was Kent!*

Wharryer mean;

Yer an Oxbridge 'Kent'?

- *No, I went to Kent,*

Yer daft cunt!

Whitsun Weddings MMXIII

(for Philip Larkin)

"When I was young..."

He paused...

"Long time ago now,

We thought *Love and Marriage*

And

Horse and carriage

Belonged together in

Time and place...

I do so, still.

Here and now I

Do not belong,

Am an alien, a time-traveller

Without a Tardis."

'A toast to:

The Bride & Groom!'

"Cheers!"

He said.

Tell me …

English schoolchildren singing:

"Where have all the flowers gone?"

Can think only of Mum

And Dad's old LP:

Marlene Returns to Germany

That husky voice:

Sag mir wo die Blumen sind…

An enclave:

Three German graves,

Left where they lay,

Athwart the neat lines

Mädchen pfluckten sie geschwind…

The scarlet haze of 'klaprozen'

On fields of green wheat beyond

The boundary wall

Blumen blühn im Sommerwind…

Those names in black columns,

Marching across the white, limestone

Surface:

Wann wird Mann je verstehen?

"When will they ever learn?"

That husk of a voice

Descending to a whisper on:

Verstehen.

(Tyne Cot cemetery, Ypres)

So much

So much

Bare

Woman-flesh

Makes

A man

Stand

Up and

Salute.

Chickville

In the lit bay

    Nestles

The fluorescent-

    Yellow

Ambulance, next

    To the

Deep-red, twin fire-

    Engines.

(After W.C.W.)

Summer of 76

Was

 Lion-skin fields

Trees

Letting fall leaves

Weeks

Ahead of autumn

Also

Me and the

Woman

On our backs

Watching

Zombie-flies circle

Lampshades

Me making her

Giggle

Blowing playfully into

Her

Sweat-damp, furry

Armpit.

That summer

Waking and finding

You not beside me

Running in panic out

Into the dawn

Light

Coming toward me through

The tall dry grass

Fingers combing seed from stalk

You in that wheat-coloured

Gown made translucent

By the sun

Rising.

Your face radiant

Haloed

That summer

Then and

Now and

Always!

The Edge

Darkness @ the edge of Dawn

Lifts,

Torches lead to the cliff-

Lip;

Beyond, sea-sound, below

Drop

Sheer to shingle.

The two pledge:

To Earth, beneath their feet;

To Air, above their heads;

To Water, out there

And

To the Fire,

A bright, child's balloon,

Rising from the Sea,

Turning white cliffs

Rose-pink, making

The wedding-guests

Blink.

Cathedral

Ding-dong, ding-dong, dang!

Peals falling as leaves,

                    In autumn.

Ding-dong, ding-dong, ding-dong, ding!

From the cathedral's

                    Lacy tower.

Falling on streets and

                    Paved squares.

Falling, falling,

                    Falling.

Calais-Fréthun

Solitary French 'soldat',

Pacing in the rain,

Machine-gun at the ready:

"Je vous saluez!

Joyeux Noël

Et

Bonne Année!"

(from the Eurostar)

C'est la vie!

It's all about
    Loss
    And
Immortality:
Rien d'autre!

How it all ends

It all ends as:

A faded gentian

Pressed between leaves

Of long ago.

(for D.H.L.)

Why not?

Why not

Become a Belgian?

You've been here

So long you

Almost are one!

I want to answer:

My own fell on me

With my birth

Was not taken

With an oath.

Instead sing:

In spite of all temptation

To join another nation

I remain an Englishman...

Turn away the question

Into laughter

Unanswered.

1/7/16

In the gap between

The bombardment's cease

And the whistle's shrill,

They heard the lark sing.

Born forty years later – to the day –

Waking on my birthday at dawn,

Think – sometimes – I hear it too.

Walk on

Walk on ashes

Walk on diamonds

Walk on water

Walk on lace

When you walk through the bloody wall

I'll know still that angel-face!

Reel good!

Whaddaya mean:

'Au-then-tic

Country Music?'

Johnny Cash:

Long Black Veil –

That's what I

"Mean!"

Jolie Laide

She certainly is and

It'd sure be

Jolly to

Lay her –

N'est ce pas?

3 into 1 does go!

That 3 transparencies

Make 1 colour

Print – This

I learned from

My father

So ...,

So,

    Deftly barefoot

To

    Your bed

The

    Rest better

Left

    Unsaid!

In the picture by Giotto

In the picture by Giotto,

Francis stands

Preaching to the birds

Perched attentively

On the branches of the

Forest trees.

Palms raised,

His first words are:

"Brothers and Sisters…"

(After William Carlos Williams:

Pictures from Brueghel)

Ladies' Night

(November 1963)

Tom Jones

(the movie, not the man)

    At

The Perrymount

Cinema –

A rare 'Ladies'

    Night'

For Mum and our

    Neighbour,

Daphne.

Dad and me are still in bed

    When

She goes down

    To

Make the morning-tea,

    Sees

The paper on the mat

    And

Calls upstairs:

    "Christ! –

They've shot Kennedy!"

Sing *Solo* for me

Sandy from shadow steps

And sings –

No dumpy, hyper

Girl more, but

Straw-hatted angel

In a ground-sweeping dress:

With no thought of leaving.

In song

Shadows pass

And

Legends live.

The Dead and the Quick

How the Dead

Look back

Out of old photographs,

Challenging the Quick with their:

"So what?"

Seen from a train

Amid the corn

A stork's saurian silhouette

In morning light.

Klaproos

On short-lived

Spoil-heaps

Poppies blow

As they did once

Elsewhere and

Long ago.

Life's just not fair!

He thought he was safe,

You see.

A car's by far the

Safest place to be

When lightning's

In the air.

But not, it seems,

When parked

Beneath a tree!

Nobel thoughts

Think of Heaney

In that Delphic pub,

Seeing it coming –

The way Joey did

In Little Italy –

Bracing for the blow:

"Fear not!"

Four reasons to dislike

Mr Eliot (TS)

If not

For his sneering dismissal

Of Lawrence;

If not

For his urbane distaste

For democracy;

If not

For his elite embrace

Of mystical Reaction;

Then for this:

"The rats are underneath the piles.

The Jew is underneath the lot."

Photographic memory

There is a lake

In the picture;

Beyond, a baroque

Castle – now ruinous

And

You, half-smiling,

In black and white,

Standing where I'm

Now standing for

Another picture –

In colour this time –

Taken with a phone.

A story by Nabokov

At

The show of paintings

From 'Old Russia',

The

Depressive émigré

Tears open door upon

Door,

In despairing search

For the past, until

One

Yields up the snowy

Streets of Petersburg

Before

The flood.

One

Day, I shall open

A door somewhere,

Step

Onto the windswept plain

Of a 60s, concrete

Shopping precinct and

Breathe free.

Richard Tagart

Richard Tagart lived in Antwerp for almost thirty years, but now lives in the South-East of England. He is the author of a short story collection:

Turning The Corner And Other Stories (2015)

A collection of his longer poetry is in preparation.

Rich-Tea Editions 2017

Proof

23/05/17

Made in the USA
Columbia, SC
22 April 2017